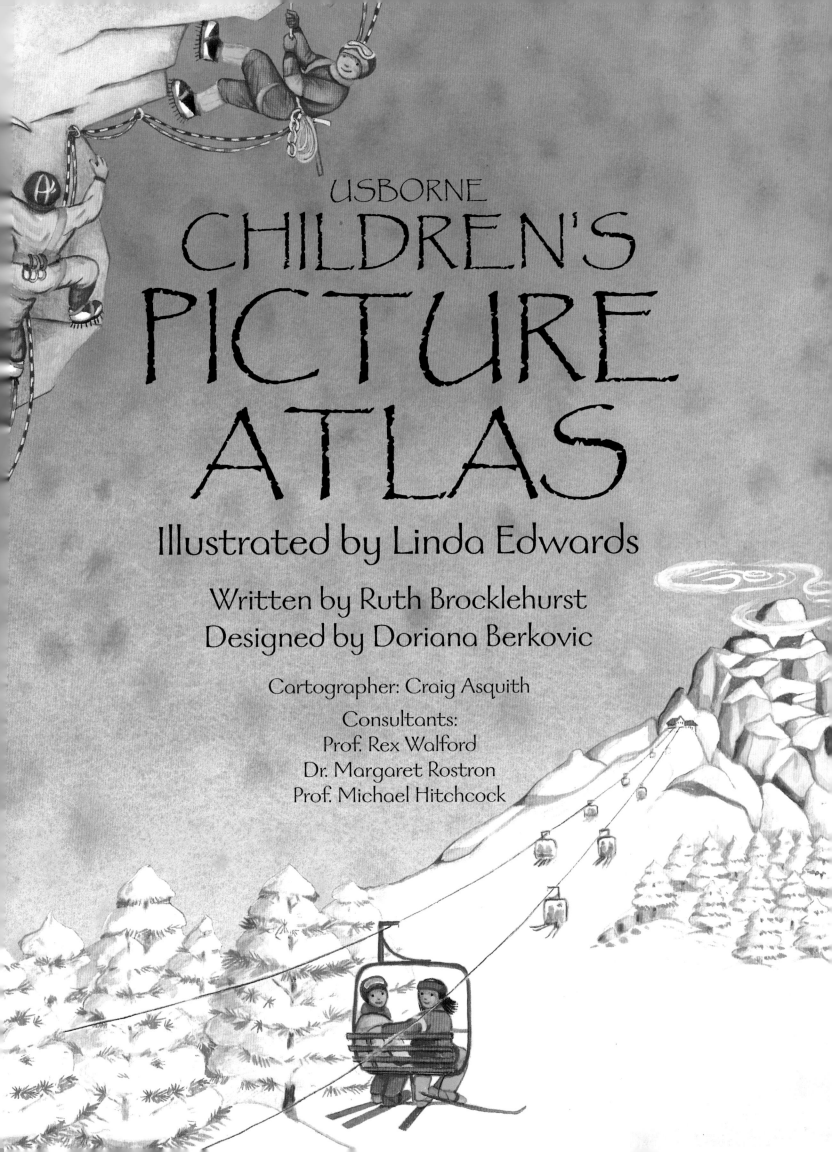

USBORNE
CHILDREN'S
PICTURE
ATLAS

Illustrated by Linda Edwards

Written by Ruth Brocklehurst
Designed by Doriana Berkovic

Cartographer: Craig Asquith

Consultants:
Prof. Rex Walford
Dr. Margaret Rostron
Prof. Michael Hitchcock

Contents

The Universe

We live in a Universe that's so enormous it's almost impossible to imagine. To picture it, you need to start small, then think big.

A town has streets with houses, shops, schools and other buildings.

Towns and cities

People live in all kinds of places around the world. Most people live in houses or apartments in towns. Really big towns are called cities.

Countries

The land around the world is divided into different countries. Countries usually have towns, cities, farmland and wild countryside.

This small country has towns, fields, mountains and sandy beaches. Not all countries are islands like this one.

Planet Earth

A country is just a small part of the land on the planet Earth. The Earth is a huge ball of rock floating in space. Land covers part of it and the rest is sea.

The Sun is a star. It gives out light and heat.

Mercury

Earth

Venus

Mars

Jupiter

Uranus

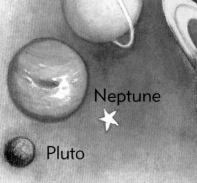

Neptune

Pluto

Saturn

This picture shows all the planets in the Solar System, and Pluto, which scientists now call a dwarf planet.

The Solar System

The Earth is one of nine planets that go around the Sun. Together, the Sun and these planets are called the Solar System. The Earth is the only planet where people, plants and animals live.

The Universe

There are trillions of stars shining in space and the Sun is one of them. A large group of stars is called a galaxy. The Sun belongs to a galaxy called the Milky Way. All the galaxies in space make up the Universe.

On a clear night, you can see thousands of stars.

5

What are maps?

Maps are pictures that show places as they look from above. They usually make places look much smaller than they really are. A book, like this one, full of maps is called an atlas.

Spacecraft called satellites are used to take photographs of the Earth from space.

Making maps

Mapmakers often use photographs of places taken from above to help them draw maps. They also measure the ground to find out the sizes of places and how far they are from each other.

This is a satellite photograph. It shows part of London.

What maps show

When mapmakers draw maps, they just include the important details. Maps often have shading, labels and little pictures to tell you more about a place.

This is a picture map of the same place as the photograph above.

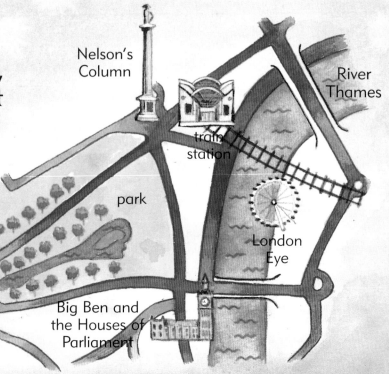

Nelson's Column

River Thames

train station

park

London Eye

Buckingham Palace

Big Ben and the Houses of Parliament

The round Earth

Because the Earth is a ball shape, a photograph can only show one side of it. Mapmakers can show the whole Earth, as it actually looks, by making a model of it. A model Earth is called a globe.

This satellite photograph shows one side of the Earth from space.

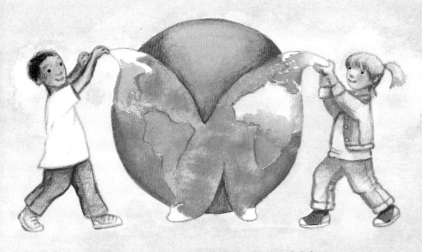

If the surface of a globe could be peeled off, this is how it would look.

Peeled Earth

To make a flat map of the round Earth, mapmakers draw the Earth as though its curved surface has been peeled off and opened out flat.

Filling the gaps

The peeled map isn't much use because it has lots of gaps. Some parts have to be squashed or stretched to make a map without gaps.

This is a peeled map. You can see a world map without gaps on pages 28–29.

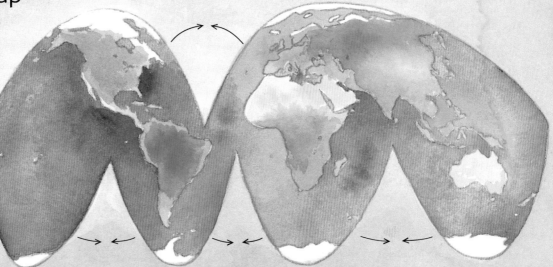

7

Countries and cities

There are more than 190 countries in the world. The place where one country meets another is called a border. On the maps in this book, the borders are shown as red dotted lines.

Borders

Many country borders are along rivers or mountains. Sometimes, borders are marked by fences or walls.

Some borders have gates where guards check who goes in and out.

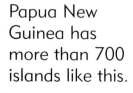

Papua New Guinea has more than 700 islands like this.

Island groups

Some countries, such as Papua New Guinea, are made up of lots of islands. The maps in this book show their borders in the sea around the islands.

Can you find these things on the maps?

Big Ben

Parthenon

St. Basil's Cathedral

Forbidden City

Eiffel Tower

Big cities

Big cities can be very crowded. Many people work or live in tall buildings called skyscrapers. The black circles ● on the maps show where the biggest cities are.

Skyscrapers can fit many hundreds of people into a small space.

This is the White House, in Washington DC, USA. The President of the USA lives and works here.

Country capitals

The people in charge of a country work in a city called the capital. Lots of capitals have big, grand buildings. Capital cities are shown as black squares ■.

Street parties

In some cities, there are street parties called carnivals. People dress up and dance in the streets.

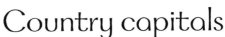

At carnivals, people wear bright, fancy costumes.

Blue Mosque

Winter Palace in St. Petersburg

Leaning Tower of Pisa

Sydney Opera House

Statue of Liberty

People

Millions and millions of people live around the world. In different parts of the world, people may look, talk and behave differently.

Japanese children wear kimonos for festivals and special occasions.

Dressing up

In some places, people dress up for special occasions in a style of clothes that people wore long ago. The clothes they wear are called traditional costumes.

Religions

A religion is a way of thinking about the world. Some people believe in one God and others believe in many gods. Most religions have holy places or buildings where people go to pray or think.

In Jerusalem, in Israel, there are many places where Christians, Muslims and Jewish people go to pray.

Can you find these people on the maps?

Guarani people

Zulu dancer

sitar player

rugby player

highland piper

Music and dancing

Many countries have their own styles of music and dancing. Some places have their own traditional musical instruments too.

Flamenco is a Spanish style of dancing to guitar music.

Chinese people often eat using chopsticks.

Eating

People around the world eat all kinds of foods. They also have many ways of cooking and eating. Food is transported long distances, so people can taste dishes from all around the world.

Sharing interests

Although people can be very different, they also have lots in common. With travel, television, telephones and the Internet, it's easy for people to share ideas.

People from all around the world get together to play soccer.

conga drummer

Tibetan monks

Hopi dancer

girl in a poncho

American football player

Getting around

There are many ways to get from one place to another. Journeys can be made by air, land or water. Some are quicker than others.

Jumbo jet planes can carry more than 600 people.

Long distances

Planes and trains can carry lots of people at a time. They make long journeys, at great speeds, all around the world.

This Japanese bullet train's shape helps it go faster.

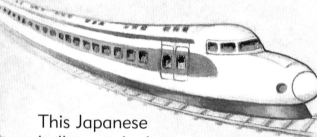

River rides

It is difficult to build roads in thick forests. The easiest way to travel there is along a river.

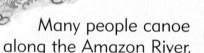

Many people canoe along the Amazon River.

Can you find these things on the maps?

basket boat

desert truck

traditional junk (boat)

Trans-Siberian Express

helicopter

Pedal power

In the busy city streets of India and China, many people use bicycles and rickshaws, instead of cars.

Rickshaws are pulled by people on foot or on bicycles. They are small, so they don't get stuck in traffic jams.

Children can ride on the back of a snowmobile.

Icy journeys

In snowy places, people use snowmobiles and sleds to get around. Snowmobiles have skis, instead of wheels, so they glide easily over the snow.

Watery city

A canal is a man-made river. In Venice, in Italy, there are canals instead of roads. People there use boats to get around the city.

Many people in Venice ride in boats called gondolas. They use poles to push the gondolas along.

Ice and snow

The white parts of the maps show places that are covered with ice and snow. The coldest places in the world are the Arctic in the north and Antarctica in the south.

Arctic terns spend half the year in the Arctic and the other half in Antarctica.

The poles

The most northern place on Earth is called the North Pole. Whichever way you go from there is south. The South Pole is on the other side of the world.

Poles apart

Penguins and polar bears never meet in the wild. This is because penguins live in Antarctica and polar bears only live in the Arctic.

Penguins huddle together to keep out the cold.

Polar bears have thick fur to keep them warm.

Can you find these things on the maps?

ice fish

humpback whale

American science station

Arctic fox

Saami people

These Inuit children are dressed in traditional parkas.

Keeping warm

People in frozen lands need to wrap up warm outside. Inuit people, who live in the Arctic, wear thick coats called parkas to keep out the cold.

Science in the snow

Antarctica is a large, cold island. There, scientists from all over the world work in science stations. They go there to study the weather and to find out about the animals that live there.

Scientists can measure how cold it is in the sky by fixing a thermometer to a weather balloon.

Icebreaker ships are strong and heavy. They break up the frozen ocean, clearing a way for other ships.

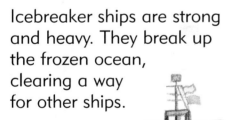

Frozen sea

There isn't any land at the North Pole, but much of the sea is frozen solid all year. In the summer, some of the ice melts and breaks up into huge chunks called icebergs.

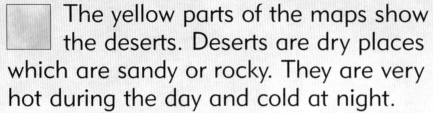

Deserts

The yellow parts of the maps show the deserts. Deserts are dry places which are sandy or rocky. They are very hot during the day and cold at night.

Flamingos flying over the Atacama Desert.

In sandy deserts, wind blows the sand into hills called dunes.

Desert records

The Sahara, in Africa, is the biggest, hottest desert in the world. The driest desert is the Atacama, in Chile. In parts, it hasn't rained for 400 years.

Oasis

An oasis is a place in the desert where there is water. Plants grow there and animals and people go there to drink.

These people are collecting water from an oasis.

Can you find these animals on the maps?

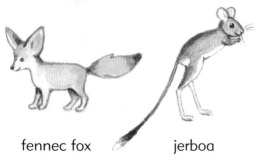

fennec fox   jerboa   blue-tongued skink   scorpion   rattlesnake

Thirsty animals

Camels can drink lots of water at once, then go for a week without any. They are suited to life in the desert in other ways too.

Camels can close their nostrils to stop sand from blowing in.

They have wide feet so they don't sink into the sand.

Plant survival

Desert plants have different ways of surviving in such dry places.

Many desert flowers only burst into bloom just after it rains.

Cactus plants store water in their stems.

Desert people

Many desert people don't live in one place. They move around with their animals, to find water and food.

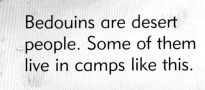

Bedouins are desert people. Some of them live in camps like this.

Grasslands

Grasslands are flat, open spaces where lots of grasses grow. They are shaded in pale green on the maps. Different types of grasses grow in different places around the world.

Safaris

The grassland in Africa is called the savanna. In the hot, dry season, the grass is dry and golden. People go on tours called safaris to see the wild animals that live there.

Lions spend most of their time resting.

Eating grass

Many savanna animals, such as zebras and antelopes, are grass-eaters. They live in large groups so they are safer from hunters, such as lions.

A group of zebras is called a herd.

Can you find these animals on the maps?

kangaroos   guanaco   buffalo   giraffe   meerkats

Green, green grass

In Northern Europe and New Zealand, the weather is often cool and rainy. The grass there is lush and green and good for cows and sheep to eat.

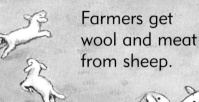

Farmers get wool and meat from sheep.

Cowboys called gauchos round up cows on horseback.

The pampas

The grassland in South America is called the pampas. Farmers there keep thousands of cows on farms called ranches. Cows are kept for meat and milk.

Grassland farming

Most of the world's wheat and corn grows on the grasslands in Russia and North America. Farmers there use big machines to collect the grain.

Combine harvesters are huge machines that cut wheat and other crops.

lion   giant anteater

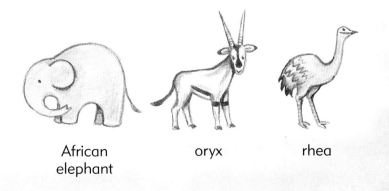

African elephant   oryx   rhea

Forests

The dark green parts of the maps show where forests are. Different types of forests grow in different parts of the world.

Conifer trees

Coniferous forests grow in cold places, with snowy winters. Conifer trees have long, thin leaves, called needles. They stay green all year round.

Conifer trees grow seed cones that squirrels eat.

More kinds of plants live in rainforests than anywhere else.

Tropical rainforests

Rainforests grow in parts of the world where it is hot and rainy all the time. They are steamy places with towering trees, thick bushes and millions of animals.

Can you find these things on the maps?

blue morpho butterfly   armadillo   red fox   raccoon   anaconda

Trees in winter

In places with mild weather, many trees lose their leaves in the winter. The leaves turn red and golden before they fall.

The winter wind blows dead leaves from the trees.

In the spring, fresh green leaves grow.

How old is a tree?

You can find out the age of a tree by counting the number of rings in its trunk. A tree has a ring for each year of its life.

When a tree is cut down, you can see the rings in its trunk.

Giant pandas only eat bamboo.

Forests of bamboo

Giant pandas live in bamboo forests, in the mountains of China. There, the bamboo grows tall and thick. Only around 600 giant pandas live in the wild.

grizzly bear

wild mushrooms

lumberjack (forester)

chimpanzee

toucan

21

Mountains

Mountains are high, rocky places. Their highest points are called peaks. Tiny mountain shapes on the maps show where the biggest mountains are.

Snowy peaks

The higher up a mountain you go, the colder and windier it gets. On the high slopes, it is too cold for trees to grow. The highest peaks are so cold that they are covered with snow, even in the summer.

Ski lifts take skiers up and down mountains.

Snow leopards have pale fur, to blend in with their snowy surroundings.

Climbing creatures

Many mountain animals, such as goats and snow leopards, are excellent climbers. They also have extra-thick fur to keep out the chilly winds.

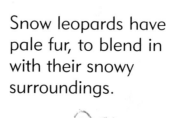

Mighty mountains

A line of mountains is called a range. The Andes, in South America, is the longest mountain range in the world.

Some farmers in the Andes keep llamas for their wool.

Climbers use ropes and hooks to help them cling onto rocky ledges upside down.

Climbing

Mount Everest is the highest mountain in the world. Many adventurers travel to Asia to make the difficult climb to its highest peak.

Condors lay their eggs where other animals can't reach them.

Mountain birds

Some birds, such as eagles and condors, live high up in mountains. They build their nests on rocky cliffs and narrow ledges.

Can you find these things on the maps?

bald eagle

Mount Everest

yak

chamois

Ural owl

Rivers and lakes

These people are using reed boats to cross Lake Titicaca.

The dark blue lines and shading on the maps show where rivers and lakes are. The water in them comes from rain and melted snow. Many towns are built near rivers and lakes and lots of animals live in and near them.

A mountain lake

The highest lake in the world is Lake Titicaca, in South America. People there make boats from reeds that grow around the lake.

A river's journey

Rivers start high up in mountains, and flow downhill into lakes or the sea. The water slowly wears away the rock to make a dip in the ground, called a valley.

The Colorado River, in the USA, flows through the world's deepest valley. It is called the Grand Canyon.

A holy river

For many people, the Ganges River, in India, is a holy place. People from around the world go there to bathe in its water.

The water in a waterfall flows fast, and looks white and frothy.

People bathe in the Ganges River during religious festivals.

A waterfall

When a river flows over a steep step in the land, the water tumbles down it and makes a waterfall.

Muddy mouths

The wide, muddy place where a river joins the sea is called the river mouth. Lots of birds live there because the mud is full of plants and tiny fish to eat.

Crocodiles and herons live by the river mouth of the Nile, in Egypt.

Can you spot these things on the maps?

capybara   piranha   Caspian seal   hippopotamus   felucca boat

Seas and oceans

More than half of the Earth is covered with the salty water of seas and oceans. There are five large oceans and lots of smaller seas. They are shown in blue on the maps.

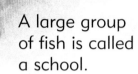

A large group of fish is called a school.

Sea life

Different types of animals and plants live in different parts of the sea. Giant squid live deep under the sea, but crabs and shrimps live in shallow water, near the shore.

Blue whales are the world's biggest animals. An adult blue whale weighs about the same as 20 elephants.

Some fishing boats have huge nets to catch fish.

Fishing

People catch fish to eat or sell. Some use fishing rods, but most fishermen go out to sea with large nets to catch lots of fish at once.

Can you find these things on the maps?

| red snappers | butterfly fish | green turtles | scuba diver | seahorses |

Tropical reefs

Coral reefs look like sea plants. In fact, they are made of thousands of tiny animals, called corals. The Great Barrier Reef, near Australia, is the biggest coral reef in the world.

Coral reefs are found in warm, shallow seas. Lots of tropical fish live there too.

Wind surfers use sails to make their boards go faster.

Sea sports

Many people enjoy swimming or splashing around near the seashore. Others go surfing on big waves, or diving under the water to look at fish.

Shipping ports

Ports are towns by the sea where ships are loaded and unloaded. Huge ships carry all kinds of things, such as food and fuel, all around the world.

Big cranes load and unload ships.

common dolphins

marlin

giant squid

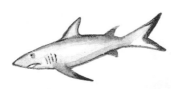

shrimps   blue shark

The world

The world is divided into seven large areas called continents. They are all named in big letters on this map.

The little pictures on this map show some world records.

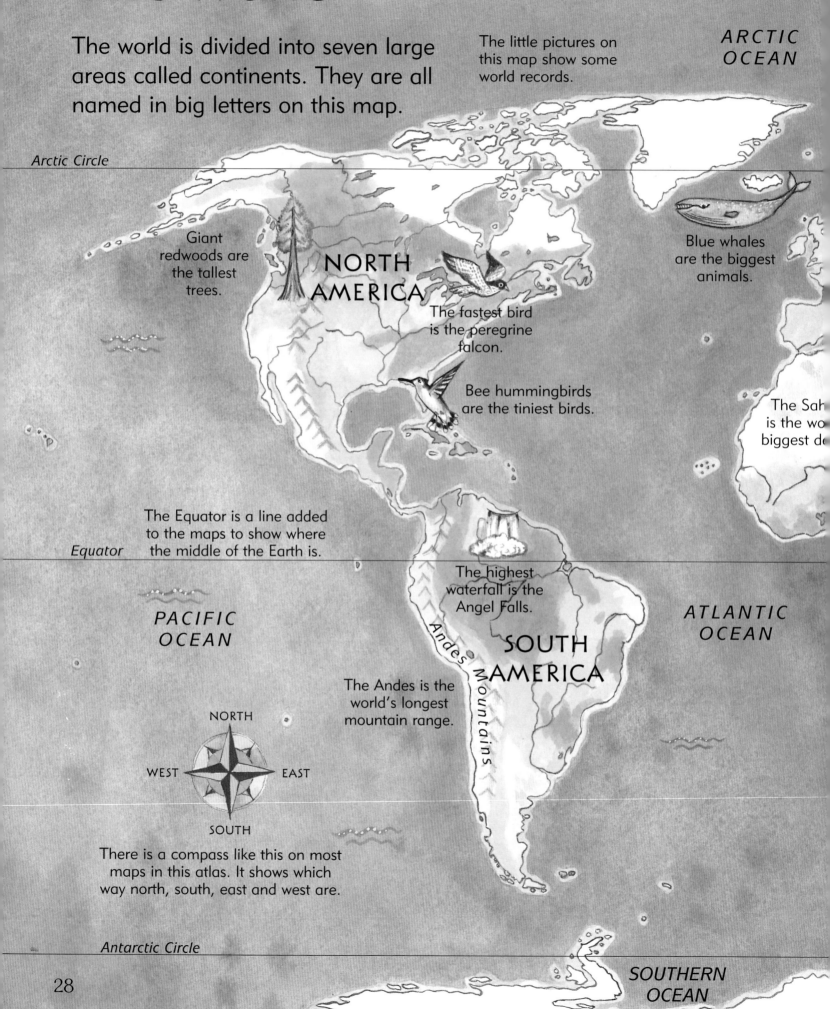

Arctic Circle

Giant redwoods are the tallest trees.

NORTH AMERICA

Blue whales are the biggest animals.

The fastest bird is the peregrine falcon.

Bee hummingbirds are the tiniest birds.

The Sah is the wo biggest d

The Equator is a line added to the maps to show where the middle of the Earth is.

Equator

The highest waterfall is the Angel Falls.

PACIFIC OCEAN

ATLANTIC OCEAN

SOUTH AMERICA

Andes Mountains

The Andes is the world's longest mountain range.

NORTH

WEST   EAST

SOUTH

There is a compass like this on most maps in this atlas. It shows which way north, south, east and west are.

Antarctic Circle

SOUTHERN OCEAN

28

The shading on the maps shows what the land is like in different parts of the world and where there are rivers, lakes, seas and oceans.

ice and snow   deserts   grasslands   forests   mountains   rivers and lakes   seas and oceans

Arctic Circle

ASIA

The Trans-Siberian Express goes along the longest train line.

ROPE

Mount Everest is the highest mountain.

PACIFIC OCEAN

HARA SERT

The Nile is the longest river.

More people live in China than in any other country.

RICA

Whale sharks are the biggest fish.

Northeast India is the rainiest place in the world.

Cheetahs are the fastest land animals.

Rafflesias are the biggest flowers.

Equator

INDIAN OCEAN

Giraffes are the tallest animals.

Uluru (Ayers Rock) is the largest rock in the world.

The biggest bird is the ostrich.

AUSTRALASIA AND OCEANIA

Antarctic Circle

Antarctica is the orld's coldest place.

ANTARCTICA

29

North America

ARCTIC OCEAN

GREENLAND

Inuit people

■ Nuuk (Godthab)

harp seal

cod

Ptarmigan

harp seal cub

boy in a kayak

igloo

minke whale

fishing boat

Labrador dog

puffins

Canada goose

snowy owl

Paper is made here.

maple

beluga whale

Hudson Bay

cloudberries

beaver

skunk

Arctic terns

wolf

Arctic hare

musk ox

moose

CANADA

mounted policeman

combine harvester

Mississouri River

arctic char

icebreaker ship

husky dog

grizzly bear

lumberjack (forester)

skier

ice hockey player

bald eagle

polar bear

snowmobile

Alaska (USA)

snow goose

muskrat

Rocky Mountains

traditional carved pole

Vancouver ●

Seattle ●

raccoon

walrus

Anchorage ●

caribou

Gulf of Alaska

Pacific salmon

PACIFIC OCEAN

killer whale

Golden Gate bridge

South America

NORTH
WEST
EAST
SOUTH

Caribbean Sea

Equator

white shark

Equator

oil rig

Caracas

VENEZUELA

iguana

hummingbird

peccary

tapir

Bogotá

COLOMBIA

Quito

EQUADOR

fruit bat

puma

Orinoco River

cow

Angel Falls

scarlet ibis

Georgetown

Paramaribo

Cayenne

rocket base

SURINAME

FRENCH GUIANA

GUYANA

arrow-poison frog

jaguar

Coffee is grown here.

brazil nuts

condor

sloth

caiman

piranha

Amazon River

Amazon Rainforest

spider monkey

Machu Picchu

Andes Mountains

llama

Lima

PERU

capybara

armadillo

toucan

blue morpho butterfly

Madeira River

orchid

parrot

Tapajós River

spectacled bear

La Paz

peanuts

BOLIVIA

Sucre

girl in

reed boat on Lake Titicaca

sardines

Guarani

cotton plant

Gold is mined here.

sugar cane

São Francisco River

bananas

conga drummer

lobster

cocoa beans

Coffee is

Brasília Cathedral

Brasília

Tocantins River

BRAZIL

anaconda

Diamonds are

shrimps

PACIFIC OCEAN

ATLANTIC OCEAN

sardines

oil tanker

carnival dancers

surfer

oranges

sardines

The world

SOUTH AMERICA

This map shows where South America is.

South Georgia

mackerel

Asunción

giant anteater

sheep ranches

URUGUAY

Montevideo

Buenos Aires

tango dancers

Paraná River

ARGENTINA

rhea

gaucho (cowboy)

chinchilla

Atacama Desert

flamingos

pelican

CHILE

Santiago

fishing boat

grapes

monkey puzzle tree

southern right whale

mackerel

killer whale

Andes Mountains

guanaco

sheep

Magellan penguin

albatrosses

Falkland Islands

sea lions

Cape Horn

rockhopper penguin

fur seal

mackerel

33

Australasia and Oceania

NORTH
WEST EAST
SOUTH

Northern
Mariana Islands

Moorish
idol

FEDERATED
STATES OF
MICRONESIA

PALAU

sea
cucumber

Equator

dugong

sacred
house

crowned
pigeon

tree
kangaroo

cuscus

PAPUA
NEW GUINEA

Port Moresby

clown fish

box
jellyfish

Great Barrier Reef

coral

butterfly
fish

pineapple
fish

Aboriginal
dancer

possum

harlequin
fish

spiny
anteater

frilled lizard

dingo

koalas

Great Sandy Desert

AUSTRALIA

blue-ringed
octopus

boy
diving for
pearls

wallaby

thorny devil

Uluru
(Ayers Rock)

kangaroos

Opals are
mined here.

platypus

bottlenose
dolphin

grass
tree

Great Victoria
Desert

Darling River

Sydney
Opera
House

flying
doctor

wombat

sheep

Sydney

parakeet

Canberra

blue-tongued
skink

emu

galah

Perth

crayfish

black
swan

Melbourne

surfer

Tasmania

sea dragon

Tasmanian
devil

great white
shark

INDIAN
OCEAN

albatrosses

sea slug

Hawaiian Islands

girl wearing a garland

surfer

jumbo jet plane

MARSHALL ISLANDS

PACIFIC OCEAN

fairy terns

angel fish

cargo ship

moray eel

NAURU

blue shark

Equator

green turtles

KIRIBATI

flying fish

SOLOMON ISLANDS

parrot fish

Tokelau

manta rays

TUVALU

fisherman in a canoe

VANUATU

coconut palms

SAMOA American Samoa

Wallis and Futuna

tuna

bananas

rugby player

coconuts

French Polynesia

New Caledonia

FIJI

TONGA

Niue

sea horses

Cook Islands

bananas

Tahiti

swordfish

snappers

barracudas

giant squid

The world

kiwi

Maori dancer

NEW ZEALAND

■ Wellington

sperm whale

AUSTRALASIA AND OCEANIA

This map shows where Australasia and Oceania are.

sheep

hoki fish

Asia

Arctic Circle

herring

fishing through ice

reindeer

kittiwake

lynx

eid du

Moscow

Volga River

Ural Mountains

maize

noctule bat

flying squirrel

man a fur h

golden eagle

honeybees

RUSSIA

Blue Mosque

Black Sea

skier

Caspian seal

space agency

Aral Sea

Astana

saiga antelope

KAZAKHSTAN

bactri cam

Istanbul

Ankara

GEORGIA

Caspian Sea

wheat

Go Des

Turkish kebabs

ARMENIA

AZERBAIJAN

UZBEKISTAN

Bishkek

jerboa

TURKEY

TURKMENISTAN

Tashkent

KYRGYZSTAN

Cyprus

SYRIA

rug

Ashgabat

TAJIKISTAN

snow leopard

Great Wa of China

LEBANON

Damascus

jackal

ISRAEL

IRAQ

Tehran

AFGHANISTAN

Jerusalem

Baghdad

Kabul

The Himalayas

Tibetan monks

JORDAN

IRAN

Islamabad

yak

hyena

KUWAIT

date palms

Afghan hound

New Delhi

Mount Everest

NEPAL

BHUTAN

oil well

PAKISTAN

Ganges River

Kathmandu

Bedouin people

QATAR

Indus River

Taj Mahal in Agra

BANGLADESH

Mecca

Riyadh

UNITED ARAB EMIRATES

Muscat

sitar player

INDIA

Dhaka

boy on elepha

water towers

SAUDI ARABIA

OMAN

girl in a sari

Bengal tiger

Nay Pyi Taw

Sana'a

Arabian horse

Red Sea

Bombay

BURMA

YEMEN

Arabian camel

Arabian Sea

rickshaw

or

Andaman Islands

Bangko

Socotra

NORTH

sacred cow

tea plant

floating market

WEST

EAST

Arabian fishing boats

Sri Jayewardenepura Kotte

SRI LANKA

SOUTH

Colombo

Kuala Lump

Equator

oil tanker

MALDIVES

coral reef

INDIAN OCEAN

rhinoce

soldier fish

tiger shark

snappers

beluga whale

narwhal

polar bears

Bering Sea

giant kelp forest

bowhead whales

ringed seal

walrus

mming

Lena River

snow goose

snowmobile

bearded seal

sperm whale

pollock

rown ear

Siberian tiger

Sea of Okhotsk

sea lion

fishing boat

wild mushrooms

Trans-Siberian Express

PACIFIC OCEAN

ger (tent)

Kites are made here.

crested puffin

girl in a kimono

bullet train

puffer fish

white-sided dolphin

an Bator

IGOLIA

Forbidden City

Vladivostock

NORTH KOREA

Beijing ■

Yellow River

Pyongyang ■

Seoul ■

JAPAN

Tokyo ■

racotta Army

rice plants

SOUTH KOREA

CHINA

Yangtze River

pagoda

crane

sumo wrestler

nt nda

bamboo

■ Taipei

traditional junk (boat)

TAIWAN

octopus

The world

NAM

Hanoi ■

Hong Kong

South China Sea

dugong

ASIA

ntiane

LAND

Manila

Philippine Sea

BODIA

om nh

basket boat

THE PHILIPPINES

manta ray

This map shows where Asia is.

AYSIA

BRUNEI

pineapples

GAPORE

Borneo

giant clam

Equator

atra

Celebes

orang-utan

rafflesia flower

coconut palms

cowrie shells

rubber trees

■ Jakarta

INDONESIA

Java

temple

EAST TIMOR

New Guinea

Arafura Sea

Africa

Mediterranean Sea

■ Algiers   ■ Tunis

Madeira   lemons   TUNISIA

Rabat ■   Tripoli ■

Atlas Mountains   olives

MOROCCO   LIBYA

spic

ATLANTIC
OCEAN

Canary Islands

Laáyoune ■   Berber
people   oasis

WESTERN
SAHARA   ground
squirrel   date
palm   ALGERIA
Sahara Desert   desert tr

bottlenose
dolphin   MAURITANIA   MALI   scorpion

ge

fisherman   Nouakchott ■   camel train   NIGER

hippopotamus   Niger River

CAPE VERDE
ISLANDS   SENEGAL
Dakar ■   baboon   CH

THE GAMBIA   BURKINA
FASO   Niamey ■   N Djam

GUINEA-BISSAU   Bamako ■   round
houses

GUINEA   BENIN   Abuja ■

Conakry ■   bananas   cocoa beans   TOGO   NIGERIA

Freetown ■   Yamoussoukro   bee-eater

SIERRA LEONE   ● Lagos

Monrovia ■   IVORY   Accra ■   Banç

cargo ship   LIBERIA   COAST   GHANA   Yaoundé ■

EQUATORIAL   CAMEROON

conger eel   GUINEA   CONG

Equator   SAO TOMÉ &
PRINCIPE   Libreville ■
GABON

ATLANTIC OCEAN   Brazza

chimpanzee   Kins

flying fish   Luanda ■   ANGOLA

oryx

cruise ship   meerkats

The world

anchovies

NAMI

AFRICA   Windhoek ■

This map shows where Africa is.

great white
shark   ost

38   Ca,
Tow

fishing boat

Cairo

pyramids

well

EGYPT

felucca
boat

Nile River

Red Sea

Nubian
Desert

hec
x

gourd

crocodile

Khartoum

ERITREA

Asmara

SUDAN

acacia
tree

ETHIOPIA

DJIBOUTI

tortoise

Addis
Ababa

SOUTH
SUDAN

hoopoe

TRAL
CAN
BLIC

rhinoceros

sugar
cane

lobelia

SOMALIA

INDIAN
OCEAN

Arab fishing
boats

NORTH

JUBA

coconut
palms

EMOCRATIC
UBLIC OF THE
CONGO

UGANDA

zebra

coffee
beans

Mogadishu

WEST

EAST

Kampala

Lake
Victoria

Congo River

SOUTH

Equator

KENYA

Nairobi

cow fish

orilla

RWANDA

lion

BURUNDI

Zanzibar
butterfly fish

frigate bird

TANZANIA

Dodoma

Dar es Salaam

SEYCHELLES

mandrill

African
elephant

cloves

hammerhead
shark

vulture

cheetah

MALAWI

Lilongwe

oriental
sweetlips fish

ZAMBIA

Lusaka

Zambezi River

ffe

Harare

aardvark

aye-aye

ZIMBABWE

MOZAMBIQUE

baobab
tree

Antananarivo

Victoria Falls

MADAGASCAR

MAURITIUS

OTSWANA

lahari
esert

octopus

orone

sunbird

Pretoria

ring-tailed
lemur

nnesburg

SWAZILAND

emfontein

Zulu dancer

Maputo

LESOTHO

jellyfish

SOUTH

39

AFRICA

pes

Europe

ARCTIC OCEAN

Arctic Circle

ICELAND

Reykjavik ■

hot mud pool

killer whale

blue whale

cod

Faroe Islands

ATLANTIC OCEAN

humpback whale

oil rig

fjord

skier

NORWAY

Oslo ■

wooden church

Shetland Islands

WEST

NORTH

EAST

SOUTH

salmon

fishing boat

highland piper

gannets

DENMARK
Copenhagen

Irish dancer

UNITED KINGDOM

North Sea

Dublin ■
IRELAND

sheep

pig   wind

NETHERLANDS

Amsterdam ■

Stonehenge

Big Ben

London ■

The Hague

Cars are made her

cargo ship

ferry

Eden project

Brussels ■

BELGIUM

GERMANY

LUXEMBOURG   Prague

apples

Paris ■

Eiffel Tower

grapes

Bern ■

castle

AUS

mussels

SWITZERLAND

FRANCE

oysters

Bay of Biscay

croissants

The Alps

ITALY

SLOV

skier

PORTUGAL

art gallery in Bilbao

lavender

skier

Leaning Tower of Pisa

gon
in Ve

Belem Tower

Madrid ■

church in Barcelona

cruise ship

Corsica

Rom

Lisbon ■

SPAIN

bull fighter

Sardinia

St Peter'
the Vatic

swordfish

cork oak tree

oranges

flamenco dancer

sardines

grapes

Mediterranean Sea

Sicily
vo

Madeira

Balearic Islands

40 Canary Islands

MA

Saami people

reindeer

puffins

flounder

fishing through ice

Arctic hare

capercaillie

wolverine

Siberian chipmunk

SWEDEN

wild mushrooms

lynx

sparrow hawk

Ural owl

Ural Mountains

FINLAND

Paper is made here.

sable

ballet dancers

wheat

Baltic Sea

moose

beaver

RUSSIA

Helsinki

Winter Palace in St. Petersburg

gymnast

wild horses

Stockholm

Tallinn

ESTONIA

sprats

LATVIA

Riga

red fox

Moscow

St. Basil's Cathedral

maize

Volga River

cow

LITHUANIA

Vilnius

potatoes

black stork

Ships are made here.

Minsk

BELARUS

wild boar

Russian dolls

balalaika player

Caspian Sea

POLAND

Warsaw

deer

Kiev

Dnieper River

Cossack dancer

Don River

European bison

brown bear

chamois

UKRAINE

CZECH REPUBLIC

SLOVAKIA

Carpathian Mountains

MOLDOVA

sunflowers

Vienna

Bratislava

Budapest

castle

Chisinau

HUNGARY

ROMANIA

space telescope

The world

Zagreb

CROATIA

Belgrade

Bucharest

EUROPE

BOSNIA & HERZEGOVINA

SERBIA

Danube River

Black Sea

sturgeon

Sarajevo

MONTENEGRO

KOSOVO

BULGARIA

Fortress in Dubrovnik

Pristina

Sofia

grapes

Istanbul

This map shows where Europe is.

MACEDONIA

TURKEY

Tirana

ALBANIA

olives

GREECE

Athens

Parthenon

Crete

olives

fishing boat

41

The Arctic

Bering Sea

fishing boat

volcanoes

Sea of Okhotsk

Gulf of Alaska

walrus

bearded seal

snowmobile

Chukchi tent

Alaska (USA)

Chukchi Sea

moose

Wrangel Island

purple heron

Siberian tiger

husky racer

wolf

CANADA

polar bear

Beaufort Sea

Arctic loon

New Siberia Islands

RUSSIA

ARCTIC OCEAN

Laptev Sea

snowy owl

salmon

narwhal

lynx

Canada goose

Arctic fox

Arctic terns

helicopter

Severnaya Zemlya

lemming

stoat

Arctic hare

North Pole

Kara Sea

Ellesmere Island

ringed seal

explorer

Franz Josef Land

Novaya Zemlya

Baffin Island

Arctic poppies

caribou

polar bear

Arctic chars

GREENLAND

harp seal

satellite station

Svalbard

Barents Sea

Arctic Circle

boy in a kayak

Nuuk (Godthab)

musk ox

minke whale

The world

THE ARCTIC

ptarmigan

puffins

cod

Reykjavik

ICELAND

ANTARCTICA

The Arctic and Antarctica are on opposite sides of the world.

ATLANTIC OCEAN

ferry

fishing boat

Antarctica

South Georgia

ATLANTIC OCEAN

SOUTHERN OCEAN

wandering albatrosses

cruise ship

Weddell Sea

robot submarine

macaroni penguin

scientist with a weather balloon

British science station

krill

Adélie penguins

sea bass

blue whale

snail fish

INDIAN OCEAN

leopard seal

Ronne Ice Shelf

Antarctic Peninsula

South America is this way.

Weddell seal

chinstrap penguin

ANTARCTICA

fur seal

rockhopper penguin

brittle star

Antarctic Circle

gentoo penguins

snowmobile

South Pole

American science station

caterpillar truck

elephant seal

Transantarctic Mountains

ski plane

krill

emperor penguins

Ross Ice Shelf

Ross Sea

ice fish

soft coral

king penguin

blue-eyed shag

French science station

Australian science station

giant petrels

krill

cod

PACIFIC OCEAN

porbeagle shark

SOUTHERN OCEAN

killer whale

Arctic terns

Africa is this way.

Australia is this way.

43

A trip around the world

Are you ready for a trip around the world? Look back through this book and try this fun quiz to find out. The answers are all on page 48.

Packing your bags

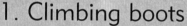

You'll need to pack carefully for your trip. Can you match these things to the places where you'll need them?

1. Climbing boots
2. A warm coat
3. A water bottle
4. A diving suit

a. The Arctic
b. Mount Everest
c. The Atacama Desert
d. The Great Barrier Reef

Things to see

1. Would you see penguins in the Arctic or in Antarctica?

2. In which town in Italy would you see canals instead of roads?

3. Which is the only country where you can see koalas and kangaroos in the wild?

4. Which city in Brazil would you visit to see people dressed up for a carnival?

Country shapes

Here are the shapes of some of the countries you might visit. Can you recognize them from the maps?

4.

1.

2.

3.

Blue clues

Can you find and name all of these things with "blue" in their names?

1. A butterfly that lives in the Amazon rainforest.

2. An octopus that swims near Australia.

3. An Australian lizard with an unusual tongue.

4. A North American bird.

People to meet

In which countries would you expect to meet these people?

1. Hopi dancer
2. Girl in a kimono
3. Reggae singer
4. Zulu dancer

45

Index of places

Index of things

Answers

Things to spot

Countries and cities
Big Ben, 40
Parthenon, 41
St. Basil's Cathedral, 41
Forbidden City, 37
Eiffel Tower, 40
Blue Mosque, 36
Winter Palace in St. Petersburg, 41
Leaning Tower of Pisa, 40
Sydney Opera House, 34
Statue of Liberty, 31

People
Guarani people, 32
Zulu dancer, 39
sitar player, 36
rugby player, 35
highland piper, 40
conga drummer, 32
Tibetan monks, 36
Hopi dancer, 31
girl in a poncho, 32
American football player, 31

Getting around
basket boat, 37
desert truck, 38
traditional junk (boat), 37
Trans-Siberian Express, 29, 37
helicopter, 42

Ice and snow
ice fish, 43
humpback whale, 40
American science station, 43
Arctic fox, 42
Saami people, 41

Deserts
fennec fox, 39
jerboa, 36
blue-tongued skink, 34
scorpion, 38
rattlesnake, 31

Grasslands
kangaroos, 34
guanaco, 33
buffalo, 30
giraffe, 39
meerkats, 38

lion, 39
giant anteater, 33
African elephant, 39
oryx, 38
rhea, 33

Forests
blue morpho butterfly, 32
armadillo, 32
red fox, 41
raccoon, 30
anaconda, 32
grizzly bear, 30
wild mushrooms, 37
lumberjack (forester), 30
chimpanzee, 38
toucan, 32

Mountains
bald eagle, 30
Mount Everest, 29, 36
yak, 36
chamois, 41
Ural owl, 41

Rivers and lakes
capybara, 32
piranha, 32

Caspian seal, 36
hippopotamus, 38
felucca boat, 39

Seas and oceans
red snappers, 31
butterfly fish, 34
green turtles, 35
scuba diver, 31
seahorses, 35
common dolphins, 31
marlin, 31
giant squid, 35
shrimps, 32
blue shark, 35

A trip around the world

Packing your bags
1. b. You'll need climbing boots on Mount Everest.
2. a. A warm coat will keep out the cold in the Arctic.
3. c. The Atacama Desert is the driest place on Earth, so you'll need a water bottle.

4. d. You'll need a diving suit to dive down to the Great Barrier Reef.

Places to see
1. Antarctica
2. Venice
3. Australia
4. Rio de Janeiro

Country shapes
1. New Zealand
2. Mexico
3. Australia
4. Italy

Blue clues
1. Blue morpho butterfly
2. Blue-ringed octopus
3. Blue-tongued skink
4. Blue jay

People to meet
1. USA
2. Japan
3. Jamaica
4. South Africa

Managing editor: Gillian Doherty   Managing designer: Russell Punter
The publishers are grateful to the following organizations and individuals for their permission to reproduce material.
p6 This image is an extract from the Millennium Map™ which is © getmapping.com plc; **p7** ©Tom Van Sant, Geosphere Project/Planetary Visions/Science Photo Library